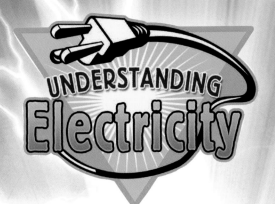

What Is Electricity?

Ronald Monroe

Crabtree Publishing Company

www.crabtreebooks.com

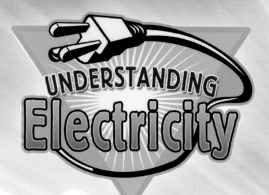
UNDERSTANDING Electricity

IMPORTANT
All experiments in this book can
be conducted by children. When
working with electricity, however, it
is always recommended that children
work with adult supervision.

Author: Ronald Monroe
Publishing plan research and development:
   Sean Charlebois, Reagan Miller
   Crabtree Publishing Company
Project development: Clarity Content Services
Editoral director: Kathy Middleon
Project management: Karen Iversen
Editor: Rachel Eagen
Copy editor: Francine Geraci
Proofreader: Crystal Sikkens
Photo research: Linda Tanaka
Design: First Image
Cover design: Margaret Amy Salter, Ken Wright
Production coordinator: Ken Wright
Prepress technician: Ken Wright
Print coordinator: Katherine Berti

Illustrations:
Chandra Ganegoda

Photographs:
cover Thinkstock, shutterstock; p1 Igor Zh./shutterstock;
p4 Samson Yury/shutterstock; p5 top Dorling Kindersley
RF/Thinkstock, iStockphoto/Thinkstock; p6 N. Mitchell/
shutterstock; p8 Lik Studio/shutterstock; p9 iStockphoto/
Thinkstock; p10 top left clockwise Brand X Pictures/
Thinkstock, sutsaiy/shutterstock, Hemera/Thinkstock,
ilker canikligil/shutterstock, Hemera/Thinkstock; p14 top
Dorling Kindersley RF/Thinkstock, Ron Monroe; p15 Ron
Monroe; p16 Dominik Michalek/shutterstock; p18
Arogant/shutterstock; p19 Stockbyte/Thinkstock; p20 top
iStockphoto/Thinkstock, NASA; p21 Vladislav Gajic/
shutterstock; p23 iStockphoto/Thinkstock; p24
Jupiterimages/Thinkstock; p25 top Hemera/Thinkstock,
Morgan Lane Photography/shutterstock; p26 Norman
Bruderhofer, www.cylinder.de/CCL/wiki; p27 Hemera/
Thinkstock; p28 top Georgi Roshkov/shutterstock, lower
left Mike Manning, Loewe AG/CCL/wiki; p29 top Mario
Roberto Duran Ortiz/CCL/wiki, Comstock/Thinkstock,
lower left Bilby/CCL/wiki, Veerachai Viteeman/
shutterstock, Luis Louro/shutterstock, mart/shutterstock.

Library and Archives Canada Cataloguing in Publication

Monroe, Ronald D.
   What is electricity? / Ronald Monroe.

(Understanding electricity)
Includes index.
Issued also in electric format.
ISBN 978-0-7787-2079-9 (bound).--ISBN 978-0-7787-2084-3 (pbk.)

   1. Electricity--Juvenile literature. I. Title.
II. Series: Understanding electricity (St. Catharines, Ont.)

QC527.2.M657 2012   j537   C2012-901504-0

Library of Congress Cataloging-in-Publication Data

CIP available at Library of Congress

Crabtree Publishing Company
www.crabtreebooks.com   1-800-387-7650

Printed in Canada/042012/KR20120316

Published in Canada
Crabtree Publishing
616 Welland Ave.
St. Catharines, ON
L2M 5V6

Published in the United States
Crabtree Publishing
PMB 59051
350 Fifth Avenue, 59th Floor
New York, New York 10118

Published in the United Kingdom
Crabtree Publishing
Maritime House
Basin Road North, Hove
BN41 1WR

Published in Australia
Crabtree Publishing
3 Charles Street
Coburg North
VIC 3058

Contents

What Do You Know About Electricity?

Isn't it rather magical that you can walk into a dark room, flip a little switch, and the room is flooded with light?

What Is Electricity?

Imagine one evening you are sitting next to a lamp doing your homework. Your brother is watching TV and your parents are cleaning up after dinner. All of a sudden, a thunderstorm begins. *Flash!* **Lightning**. *Boom!* The power goes out. You need a flashlight. You slowly shuffle across the carpet and reach for the door handle. Sparks fly between your fingers and the handle.

This might have made you curious about **electricity**.

- How does electricity work?
- What causes lightning?
- Why do sparks fly from your fingers?

What would you like to know about electricity?

How Is Electricity Defined?

Around 1600, William Gilbert, an English doctor and scientist, coined the term electricity to describe the energy created when he rubbed amber and wool together.

Did you know that absolutely everything contains electrical **charges**— even your own body? Electrical charges can be either positive or negative.

An atom is a tiny particle that is made up of **protons**, **neutrons**, and **electrons**. Protons and neutrons make up the **nucleus**, or center, of the atom. Electrons spin around the nucleus. Protons have a positive charge, electrons have a negative charge, and neutrons don't carry a charge at all. Atoms usually have the same number of protons and electrons.

A positive electrical charge develops when an atom loses one or more of its electrons to another atom. The atom that collects more electrons gains a negative charge. This buildup of extra electrons is electricity.

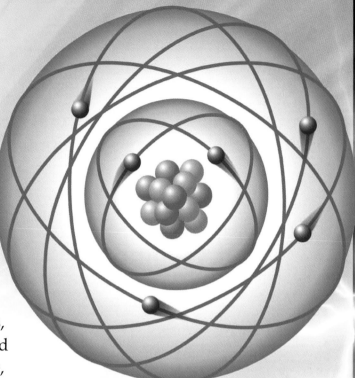

In this carbon atom, six electrons circle the nucleus with its six protons.

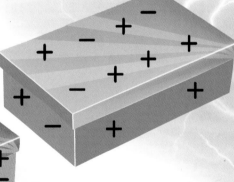

Electrons have moved from the atom on the right to the atom on the left. Extra electrons give it a negative charge. The atom on the right has more protons, so it has a positive charge.

Flash fact

Electro comes from the Greek word for amber. Amber takes an electrical charge easily. *Electro* is part of the words electricity, electron, and **electromagnet**.

What Is Static Electricity?

Static means staying in one place, not moving. Static electricity **is a buildup of electrons in the atoms of a substance, making a negative charge. You cannot see static electricity, but you can see its effects!**

Try It for Yourself!

Experiment
See some effects of static electricity.

Materials
⚡ 2 balloons, same size and shape

Procedure
1. Blow up the balloons to the same size and shape. Tie each to seal.
2. Vigorously rub each balloon back and forth against your hair for a minute. Don't let the balloons touch each other.
3. Place each balloon carefully against a wall.

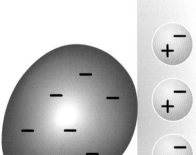

What Happened and Why
What happened? Each balloon stuck to the wall. They acted like magnets. That is because the rubbing caused electrons to move from your hair to the balloons. This gave them negative charges. The wall now has a more positive charge than the balloons. Opposite charges **attract** each other and pull the balloons against the wall.

Try It for Yourself!

Experiment
See how static electricity **repels**.

Materials
- 2 balloons, same size and shape
- 2 15-inch (30 cm) pieces of string

Procedure

1. Blow up the balloons to the same size. Tie each to seal.
2. Tie a string onto the knot of each balloon.
3. Rub one balloon again against your hair. Hold it by the string and let it hang. Don't let it touch anything else.
4. Hold the second balloon in your other hand and rub it against your hair. Hold it by the string. Don't let it touch anything.
5. Slowly move the balloons together until they are close but not touching.

Like charges repel

Repel

What Happened and Why

What happened? The balloons repelled each other. Each balloon has a negative charge from being rubbed against your hair. Same charges push each other away.

You saw the magnetic effects of static electricity, without seeing the electricity itself.

Opposite charges attract

Like charges repel

Different charges, one negative (–) and one positive (+), attract each other. Same charges, both negative (– and –) or both positive (+ and +), repel each other.

When Do You See Static Electricity?

Sometimes static electricity builds up so many electrons that it just has to move. You can see the electrons when they jump to an object with an opposite charge.

Try It for Yourself!

Experiment

See if you can be a container for static electricity.

What Happened and Why

Did a spark fly? As you shuffled, your body collected electrons and built up static electricity. As your finger neared something with an opposite charge, the electricity flowed. This created the spark. Can you remember other times when you experienced the shock of static electricity?

Procedure

1. Find a room with a wool or nylon carpet.
2. Shuffle around on the carpet for a few minutes in bare or sock feet.
3. Do not touch anything.
4. Ask a friend to reach his or her pointer finger toward you. Slowly move your pointer finger toward theirs until you almost touch. You could instead try reaching your finger toward a metal door handle.

What Is Lightning?

Lightning is a dramatic and powerful movement of static electricity. How does such a huge amount of static electricity build up?

As storm clouds grow, the wind whirls around. The motion causes big buildups of static electricity in some parts of the clouds. Lightning dancing across the sky is electrons flowing to areas of positive charge. Lightning strikes to the earth are masses of electrons flowing to the positively charged earth.

The electrons in a lightning flash are invisible. What we really see is the power of the electrons causing air to heat up so much that it creates a brilliant light.

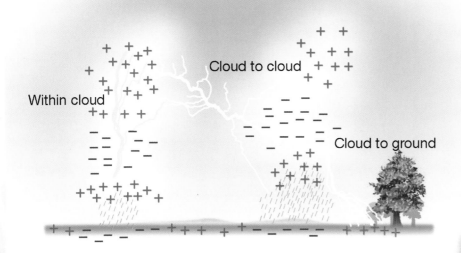

Within cloud

Cloud to cloud

Cloud to ground

Lightning flows from an area of one charge to another, within clouds, between clouds, and between clouds and the earth.

Flash fact

Lightning strikes the earth an amazing 3,000,000 or more times every day! That's a lot of static electricity on the move!

What Is Current Electricity?

Current electricity **is a flow of electrons. We are most familiar with current electricity as it flows through wires in our homes.**

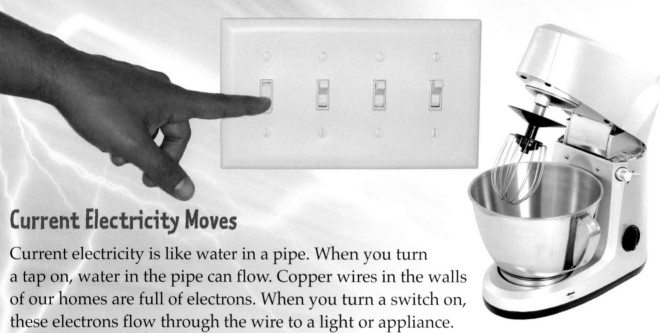

Current Electricity Moves

Current electricity is like water in a pipe. When you turn a tap on, water in the pipe can flow. Copper wires in the walls of our homes are full of electrons. When you turn a switch on, these electrons flow through the wire to a light or appliance.

As current electricity flows, it is converted, or changed, into other kinds of energy to be useful: light in a light bulb; heat in a toaster or iron; motion in a mixer or dishwasher.

What Is an Electrical Circuit?

In gym class, you might sometimes complete an exercise circuit, where you run around the gym doing different exercises. A **circuit** is a route that starts and finishes at the same place. Electrical circuits provide a route for electrons to flow from beginning to end.

This diagram shows the four parts of a simple electrical circuit.

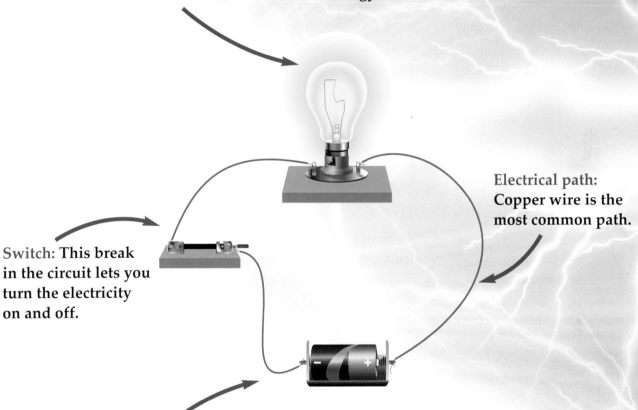

Resistance: A light, heating element, machine or other electrical device changes electrons into a different form of energy.

Electrical path: Copper wire is the most common path.

Switch: This break in the circuit lets you turn the electricity on and off.

Power source: **The battery pushes electrons into the circuit.**

Open the switch and the circuit is broken. No electrons can flow. Close the switch and the circuit is complete. Electrons can flow.

A **schematic** uses symbols to explain an idea. Look at the schematic above of the parts of a circuit. The lines represent the wires. What symbols represent the **battery**, **resistance**, and **switch**?

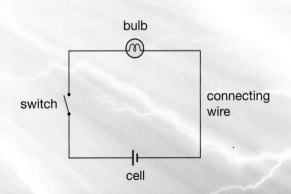

bulb

switch

connecting wire

cell

What Is Direct Current?

Direct current **is one kind of current electricity. In direct current, electrons flow in only one direction around a circuit. Direct current, or DC, usually comes from batteries.**

Try It for Yourself!

Experiment

See how common items make electricity.

Materials

- Lemon
- 1 small holiday light or other small bulb, preferably with wires attached, 1/2 inch (1 cm) of wire ends bare
- 1 long zinc screw
- 1 long copper screw

Safety

Work with an adult if you need to use any cutting tools to remove the insulation from the ends of the wires.

Procedure

1. Roll the lemon back and forth on a hard surface until it feels slightly squishy.
2. Stick the zinc screw into the lemon as shown in the diagram. Don't let it poke through the bottom.
3. Stick the copper screw into the lemon, beside (but not touching) the zinc screw.
4. Tightly wrap the end of one of the bulb's wires around the top of the zinc screw.
5. Touch the other wire against the copper screw to complete the circuit.

What Happened and Why

You should see light! Move the wire away from the copper screw. What happens? Wrap the wire around the screw and the light will stay on. The acid in the lemon reacts with the metal screws. This reaction causes electrons to flow to the zinc screw and through the wires around the circuit.

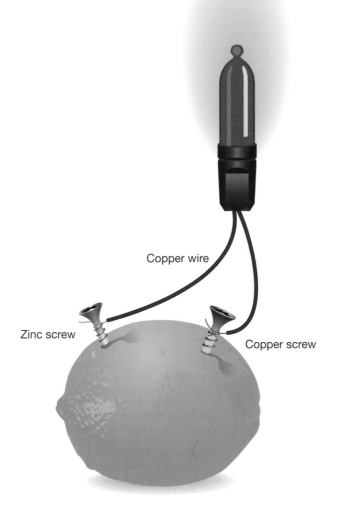

Copper wire

Zinc screw

Copper screw

Do you think other fruits and vegetables can make electricity?

How Do Batteries Work?

Cells are the simplest batteries. A battery might be one cell or many cells. Battery cells produce direct current.

Electron Flow

Batteries use reactions between metals and chemicals to create a flow of electrons. The electrons flow in one direction from the negative end of the battery. They move through a circuit and back to the positive end of the battery.

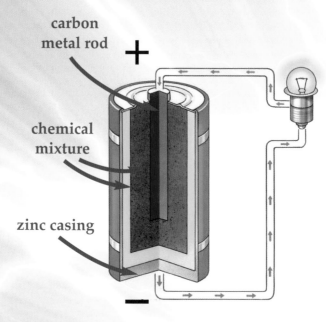

carbon metal rod

chemical mixture

zinc casing

In this battery, the chemical mixture allows electrons to flow from the positive carbon metal rod to the zinc casing where they collect and create an electrical charge. When there is a complete circuit, the electrons flow from the zinc casing, through the circuit, and back to the positive rod.

Batteries have different strengths. Letters or numbers on the sides of batteries indicate their strengths. Can you find any AA, AAA, C, or D batteries in your home?

Some items that use direct current are cameras, cars, and flashlights. Can you list other items that use batteries?

Flash fact

Cellphones, MP3s, cameras, and other electronics use rechargeable batteries. Electrons are pumped back into the batteries of these devices when they are plugged in.

How Is Electricity Measured?

Electrons are always flowing. Different instruments and units of measure have been invented to measure the power and force of electrical currents.

Voltage (V) is a measure of the pressure that forces electrons through a wire.

Resistance is a measure of how much a substance slows electrical current. It is measured in ohms (Ω). Copper wire has a low resistance, so it allows electrons to flow through it easily. Insulating materials, such as rubber, have a high resistance; they really slow electron flow.

The quantity of electrons (amount of electricity) moving through a wire is measured in **amperes** (A).

A **watt** (W) is a measurement of the amount of electricity used by a light or appliance in one second.

Electrical production and manufacturing of electrical equipment depend on these measurements and their relationships.

Toaster Model CT70XL /A
120V ~ 60Hz 970W
Made in China
Fabriqué en Chine

c(UL)us
LISTED
E127216
2H90

Labels on electrical equipment show how much voltage they need and how much electricity they use. This label is from a countertop oven. It requires 120 volts to work, and it uses 970 watts of electricity.

What Is Alternating Current?

Most of the electricity we use in homes, offices, and factories is alternating current.

Alternating Current

To alternate means to go back and forth. In alternating current, electrons go one direction in a circuit and then in the reverse direction. This happens so quickly that it seems like the electrons are vibrating back and forth.

Alternating current is used in power lines to carry electricity to where it is needed. Alternating current was chosen over direct current because it does not lose as many electrons over long distances.

Nikola Tesla was an American scientist who invented alternating current, by discovering how electricity and magnetism work together. He found that a moving wire in a magnetic field can generate electricity.

Nikola Tesla created interesting electrical devices. Plasma balls, like this, show how electricity reacts when fingers come near it.

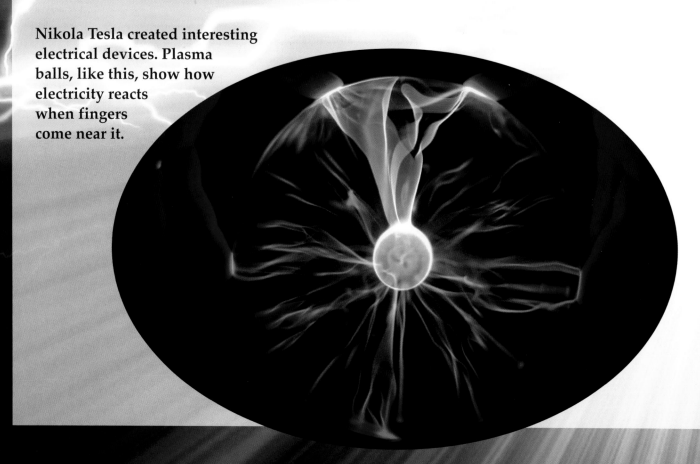

Simple Alternating Current Production

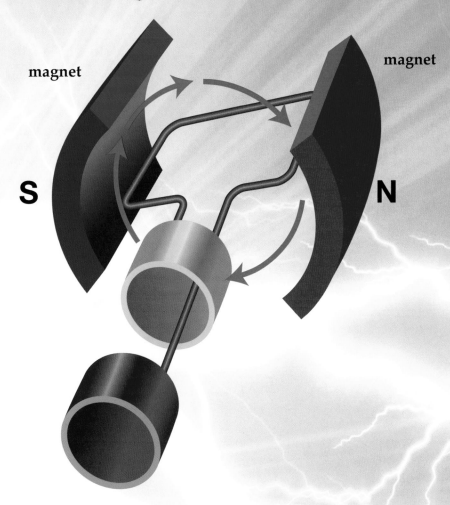

All magnets have two ends, the north pole and the south pole. When a wire loop spins between the two poles of a magnet, it collects electrons. As one side of the loop moves toward the north pole of the magnet, the electrons get pushed to move in one direction. As that side of the loop moves toward the south pole of the magnet, the electrons get pushed to move in the other direction. This creates alternating current.

Tesla built the world's first alternating current power station in the late 1800s at Niagara Falls. His partners were George Westinghouse and J.P. Morgan. Westinghouse became a major manufacturer of household appliances.

Flash fact

How Do We Produce Alternating Current?

Alternating current gets its electron flow from metal conductors and magnetic fields moving around each other.

Energy Conversion

Steam presses on the wings of the turbine. The turbine spins, allowing the generator to produce an electric current.

All of the electricity we use is created from other forms of energy. Power plants change mechanical energy (created from motion) and magnetic energy (created from a magnetic field) into electricity.

Nuclear, coal, and natural gas power plants use heat energy to turn water into steam. The pressure from the steam converts to mechanical energy, which spins turbines—machines with blades—in the **generators**.

The pressure of water behind dams or fast-moving rivers turns turbines in hydroelectric plants. In some places, the daily movement of ocean tides spins turbines to create electricity.

Windmills and wind-powered turbines change wind energy into electricity. Used for centuries, they are more popular than ever.

How Do Generators Work?

Electrical generators in power plants convert mechanical energy and magnetic energy into electrical energy.

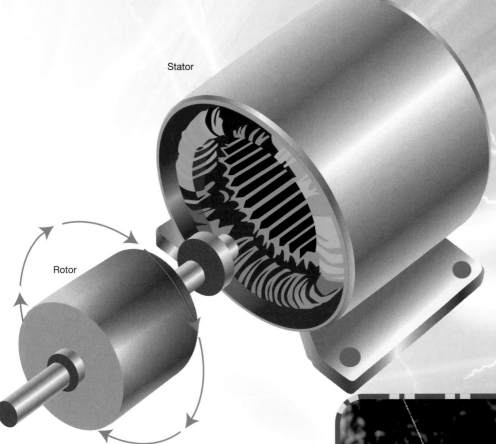

Stator

Rotor

An energy source turns a turbine. The turbine turns a **rotor** that is surrounded by a **stator**. The rotor holds a wire circuit wound around it. Electricity goes through this coil and creates an electromagnetic field. The stator contains coils of metal wires. As the rotor spins, the stator collects electrons from the moving magnetic field and pumps them into power lines to your home.

The girl pushing her friend is converting chemical energy in her body into mechanical energy in her muscles. She transfers her mechanical energy to the swing.

How Is Electricity Transported?

Electricity is transported along power lines from generating plants to businesses, factories, and our homes. This system of power lines is called the electrical grid.

The Electrical Grid

Large transmission lines carry electricity across long distances. Smaller transmission lines branch off to rural and urban areas. Power lines, above or below ground, branch off to local neighborhoods. These lines connect individual buildings to the entire **electrical grid**.

This photo of Earth at night was taken from space. Just think of the massive electrical grids that supply electricity around the Earth.

Flash fact

The power grid has **breaker** switches along the lines for safety. If a power line is hit by lightning, the surge of electrons opens the breaker. This opens the circuit so the power surge cannot follow the lines into homes and cause damage.

Your Household Wiring

The electrical grid is one large electrical circuit. The wiring in your home's walls are circuits that contain lights, outlets, and switches. Your bedroom circuit is connected to the entire power grid. When you turn on the light in your bedroom, you complete the circuit. Electrons flow from the generator at the power plant through the grid and into the circuit in your home.

This schematic shows the way a room's circuits could be wired. The circuits begin at the breaker box where wires from the electrical grid connect to your household wiring. From there it goes in the walls to every outlet (⊖=), switch (**S**), and light (◯). Each circuit is complete, connected through the grid, all the way back to the power plant.

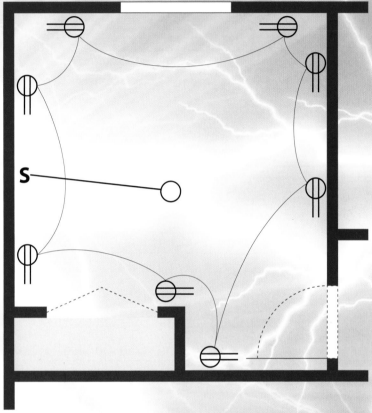

When the lamp is plugged in, the circuit is completed all the way back to the generating plant. Electricity then flows to the lamp.

How Do We Use Electricity?

Homes today are dependent on electricity for dozens of uses. Can you name some different ways that you use electricity?

Try It for Yourself!

Investigation

List all the ways you use electricity in your home.

Procedure

1. Plan how you will organize the list of electrical items in your home. It might help if you examine one room at a time.
2. Record all the electrical items you can find.
3. Organize your list into categories.

Electrical Items

My bedroom
Lamp
Light
Alarm clock
MP3
Camera
Computer

Living Room
Light
Lamps
Television
Video game
Stereo

Kitchen
Stove
Microwave
Coffee maker
Refrigerator
Toaster

How many items did you find?

How did you organize your list?

Electricity and Industry

Electricity must be changed to light, heat, mechanical, or chemical energy to be useful.

Industries use electric motors to power machines that complete many manufacturing steps. Robot welders, like those used in the auto industry, use circuits to control their movements and strong electric current to weld metals together.

Communication industries use electricity to send signals through wires or over the air. Telephones, cell phones, radio, computers, TV, and Internet all depend on electricity. Satellites transmit signals around the world, giving us instant global communication.

Some industries use electricity to cause reactions in chemicals. This creates new chemicals used in other industries, and even new medicines.

Electricity powers the movement of robots in many factories. In car assembly plants, robots lift heavy metal pieces and weld them together.

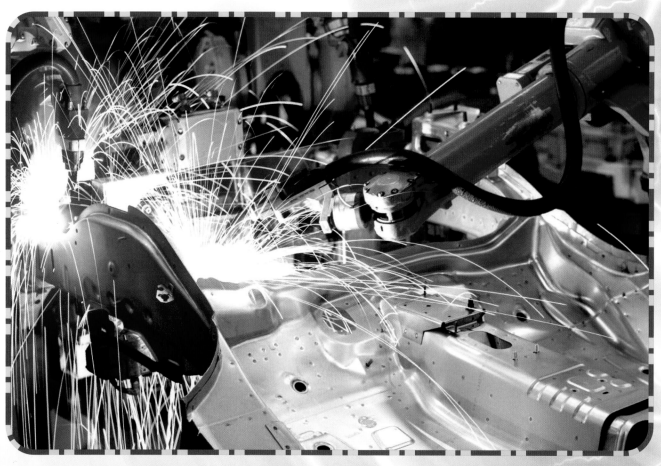

How Can You Be Environmentally Friendly?

You can help the environment by making smart choices about how you use electricity.

Producing Electricity

Electricity creates very little pollution, but producing it is another story.

- Natural gas and coal power plants release **greenhouse gases** and other pollutants into the air.
- Nuclear power plants produce dangerous nuclear waste.
- Wind turbines can kill birds and produce noise pollution.
- Dams for hydroelectric plants flood land above the dam and change the water environment below the dam.

WE
RECYCLE

Reducing Electrical Use

Here are some tips to reduce your use of electricity.

- Turn off computers, televisions, and other items when you are not using them.
- Use electricity when others are not. Most electricity is used at suppertime, so avoid using high-energy appliances then.
- Hang clothes to dry rather than using the dryer.
- Turn off lights in rooms when you are not in them.
- Let your hair dry naturally rather than using a blow dryer.
- Unplug items if you will not be using them for a few days. Many TVs and appliances continue to use electricity even when they are turned off because they are still plugged in. They are called electrical vampires.

What are other ways you can reduce your electricity use?

Thomas Edison patented his incandescent light bulb in 1880. We still use bulbs with his design. Incandescent bulbs waste electricity as they create unnecessary heat. Many people now choose energy-efficient fluorescent and LED light bulbs, which do not produce much waste heat.

Flash fact

Solar energy is environmentally friendly. Solar cells convert the unlimited energy of the Sun into direct current.

Who Made Electrical Discoveries?

Electricity today would not be the same without the contributions of these brilliant scientists. Pick one discovery and try to learn more!

Francis Hauksbee (English)—early 1700s— discovered light could be produced by sending electricity through a tube of mercury vapor. This discovery led to the fluorescent and neon lights we use today.

Benjamin Franklin (American)—mid 1700s— discovered that lightning is a form of electricity

Alessandro Volta (Italian)—early 1800s—created a simple battery and named the term volt after himself

Samuel Morse (American)—1838—invented Morse code, the first communication using electricity through wires over distance

Thomas Edison (American)—1870s— invented direct current generators and created the Edison Company to deliver electricity to homes in New York City. He also developed the first usable light bulb. He invented many electrical items, including the first phonograph (record player) and motion picture camera.

Benjamin Franklin

Thomas Edison

Alexander Graham Bell (born in Scotland, moved to Canada)—1876—invented the telephone

Nikola Tesla (born in Serbia-Croatia, moved to U.S.A.)—1870s—invented the alternating current motor. This allowed for future developments in appliances, household items, and factory engines. In 1896, he developed hydroelectric generators to produce alternating current.

Charles Parsons (English)—1884—invented first turbine

Guglielmo Marconi (born in Italy, moved to U.S.A.)—1897—sent first radio message

Nikola Tesla

What Does the Future Hold?

Some inventions and discoveries have made huge changes in our lives.

Changing Our Lives

A **silicon chip** contains many tiny electrical circuits. They turn on and off, opening and closing the circuits. Today's computers use chips to save information and perform tasks with the simple off and on action of the silicon circuits.

Years ago, computers consisted of many rooms of electrical circuits. Silicon chips have allowed for the development of smaller and smaller computers. This has given us modern devices such as MP3 players, laptops, tablets, and microwaves. Even today's cars are computerized.

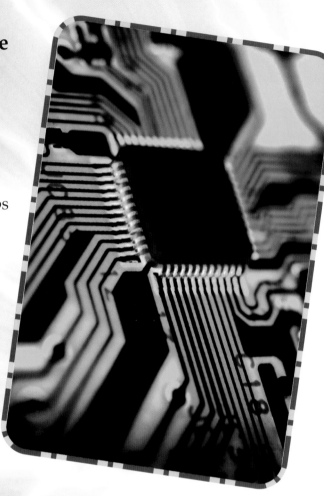

1913	1919	1928–1936	1941	1947	1951
electric refrigerator	radio receiver	first televisions	first computer	transistor—smaller, more efficient electronics	nuclear power station

And on We Go!

For the last few years, scientists have focused on solving these problems: Gasoline has become more expensive and scarce. Gasoline engines release harmful greenhouse gases.

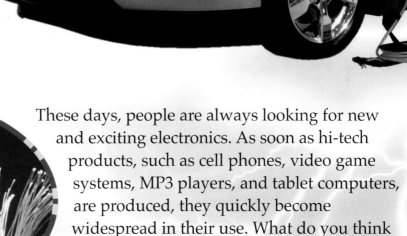

Electric vehicles could solve that problem. Scientists have worked to create stronger and longer-lived batteries. Electric cars are now more powerful and can travel farther distances between charging. One day, we might drive cars that are powered by the Sun!

These days, people are always looking for new and exciting electronics. As soon as hi-tech products, such as cell phones, video game systems, MP3 players, and tablet computers, are produced, they quickly become widespread in their use. What do you think will be the next big invention?

1961	1975	1992	1990S	2010
silicon chip	laptop computer	MP3	home Internet	tablet computer

Glossary

alternating current Electrons moving in one direction and then reversing direction

ampere A measure of amount of electricity flowing

attract Draw near, pull toward

battery A container that stores a chemical mixture that can produce electricity

breaker A switch that opens a circuit if there is an electrical surge or overload

charge An imbalance of electrons

circuit A circular route that returns to its starting point

conductor A material that electricity can pass through easily

current electricity Flowing electrons

direct current Electrons flowing in one direction

electrical grid System of wires to transport electricity around the country

electricity A buildup or flow of charged particles called electrons

electromagnet A magnet created by electricity flowing through wire

electron A negative particle circling an atom's nucleus

generator A machine that produces electrical current

greenhouse gases Harmful gases that trap heat in Earth's atmosphere

lightning A flow of static electricity from clouds to earth

neutron A particle in an atom's nucleus that has no electric charge

nucleus Center of an atom

proton A positive particle in an atom's nucleus

repel Push apart

resistance An element in a circuit that slows electrons

rotor Rotating electromagnets in a generator

schematic Diagram with symbols representing parts of a circuit

silicon chip A small square containing small electrical circuits, used in computers

static electricity Electricity that stays in one place, not moving

stator Part of a generator that does not move; collects electrons

voltage A measure of electrical force

watt A measure of how much electricity something uses in a second

Learning More

FURTHER READING

Hydroelectric Power: Power from Moving Water (Energy Revolution). Marguerite Rodger. Crabtree Publishing Company, 2010.

Inventing the Electric Light (Breakthrough Inventions). Lisa Mullins. Crabtree Publishing Company, 2007.

Using Energy (Green Team). Sally Hewitt. Crabtree Publishing Company, 2008.

What Are Electrical Circuits? (Understanding Electricity). Ronald Monroe. Crabtree Publishing, 2012.

What Are Insulators and Conductors? (Understanding Electricity). Jessica Pegis. Crabtree Publishing, 2012.

What Is Electromagnetism? (Understanding Electricity). Lionel Sandner. Crabtree Publishing, 2012.

WEBSITES

Kid Zone: Our Electricity
www.enwin.com/kids/electricity/

neoK12 Electricity   Educational Videos, Lessons, and Games for K-12 School Kids
www.neok12.com/Electricity.htm

Canada Science and Technology Museum School Zone Background Information for Electricity
www.sciencetech.technomuses.ca/english/schoolzone/Info_Electricity.cfm

You Tube Electricity for Kids
www.youtube.com/watch?v=TE5iadS9cqc

Alliant Energy Kids Fun Facts About Electricity
www.alliantenergykids.com/EnergyBasics/AllAboutElectricity/000418

Index